Upside Down

Rainbow

Alice's book gives us all hope and inspires each one to 'get after it'. She pulls you into her experience and forever changes your view of what one can do against the odds. Speed monkeys rule!

—LeAnn Puglisi, R.N., B.S.N., C.C.M.

I feel very fortunate to have had the opportunity to work with Alice as her massage therapist during a short time after such a traumatic life lesson. When I read her original patient intake I was blown away with the reality that this person was still alive and sitting in my office. Knowing what I knew about traumatic accidents, very few people could have survived with such a great attitude and smile. When you're lying in a hospital bed and you've been poked and prodded all night long to see if you're still alive, you wonder what is happening! That's when a book like this comes along to encourage you to get through the next moment.

Alice not only has captured the reality of someone dealing with the traumatic experience, she has lived it. This book is a must in guiding and encouraging the personal healing process.

—David Lang LMT, TPMT
Director of Advanced Manual Therapy, University of New Mexico, Center for Life

The world is filled with people that walk in defeat. Pain, feelings of not meeting the mark and the frustrations of this world seem to enslave them. Alice Hurst has now given us a book on victory following her personal tragedy. Her story is one of inspiration and a true testimony of how perseverance and just plain old hard work will get you through a valley in your life. Your story may not be the same but this book will certainly inspire you to move forward no matter what your personal valley is. This is a book that will make you cry, laugh and cheer her onto victory!

—Tanya Cillessen, P.T., C.W.C.E.

Mercury HeartLink
www.heartlink.com

Upside Down

Rainbow

Trauma Recovery
of Mind, Body & Spirit

Alice Hurst

Upside Down Rainbow: Trauma Recovery of Mind, Body & Spirit
Copyright ©2012 Alice Hurst

ISBN: 978-0-9854153-1-0
Publisher: Mercury HeartLink
Printed in the United States of America

All rights reserved. This book, or sections of this book, may not be reproduced or transmitted in any form without permission from the author.

Contact Alice Hurst at author@alicehurst.com

Heartfelt thanks and much love to Barry, my husband, for being strong and steady. I am grateful to my sons, Brandon and Aaron, for growing up wonderfully. Love to my mom for the late-night conversations and homemade *caldito*. I appreciate my sister, Patti, for believing in me and this book. To my loyal friend, Susan, who is always willing to share her laughter and wisdom, thank you. I will always be grateful to the Albuquerque Police and Fire Departments and the paramedic units for all you did in the first minutes after the accident. To UNM Hospital's trauma, ICU and orthopedic departments for all you did in the first days. To HealthSouth Rehabilitation Hospital staff for getting me on my feet. Thank you to all the health care professionals who had a hand in helping me heal, especially William Wellborn, M.D., Tanya Cillissen, P.T., David Lang, L.M.T., Mary Loescher, Ph.D., and Judy Borich, Ph.D.

I am appreciative to Joanne Bodin, award winning author of *Walking Fish*, for taking the time to read my manuscript and offer valuable advice and encouragement. Thanks to Jeanne Shannon for her editing skill and open heart. You made my book so much better. And finally, thank you to publisher Stewart Warren of Mercury HeartLink for his expertise, creativity, and guidance. Lastly, I have such immense gratitude for the resiliency of the human body and spirit.

Contents

ACKNOWLEDGEMENTS IX

PROLOGUE 1

INTRODUCTION 5

Memories
CHAPTER ONE 9

Change
CHAPTER TWO 19

Rehab
CHAPTER THREE 31

Journal
Chapter Four   45

Grace
Chapter Five   71

Thrive
Chapter Six   75

Live
Chapter Seven   77

Good Reads   81

About the Author   83

To all who work bravely
to find their way
back to themselves

Prologue

She lay on the pavement. Her heart racing as her body thrashed on the asphalt, struggling to stand, seemingly unaware that it couldn't. She wasn't thinking anything. Her mind and her body flooded mercifully with adrenalin. Suddenly someone was there, next to her. A young man was touching her shoulder softly. "Stay down, don't try to get up."

As if his voice had shocked her body and mind into the reality of the mysterious moment, suddenly she became aware. Aware of the car driving off. Aware of the people running toward it, pounding on the window, yelling for the driver to stop.

Then all at once, in microseconds, came the replay of the whole event. The initial hit of the front bumper that took her off balance. The turn of her head as she looked at the driver through the windshield. The beginning of panic that was in her voice as she yelled, "Hey, what are you doing?"

The sudden surge of speed that sent her body reeling to the ground. The momentary feeling of pain. The pain gone. The repetitive pounding of the pavement with her body as she tumbled uncontrollably. The groans coming from somewhere. Was it her making these unnatural guttural sounds? She was screaming, "STOP! Who are you? Why are you trying to kill me?" She was trapped somewhere, she couldn't think clearly. Then clarity. A tire. She was hypervigilant now. *Oh my God, a tire!* She dug her fingernails into the rough asphalt and pulled with all her might. A groan.

A thud as the tire climbed over her. She tumbled again. Suddenly she was free, cool air touching her skin.

A young man was asking her questions. She couldn't focus. Her body wouldn't be still.

"Tell me," he was saying. "Who are you? What's your name?"

She responded finally. Information was pouring from her mouth as though she were a human Teletype. She wanted Barry there before she died. "Alice. Tell Maria to call my husband."

The adrenalin surge was over. The pain was immense. It gripped every cell of her being. "I'm dying! Help me! Who tried to kill me?" She whimpered. She couldn't be still. Her mind and body writhed and struggled. Suddenly there was Maria. She was stroking her head. "You're OK. You'll be all right."

"Oh my God, who did this, Maria? Did someone stop them? I'm going to die! Am I going to die? I'm going to die," she both stated and asked over and over again.

"You'll be OK." Her co-worker reassured her, not sure at all that she would be.

My son! she thought. She was trying to remember what he was wearing when he had left for high school that day. *Was this morning the last time I'd see him?* she wondered. Her other son was in Utah. It seemed so far away. "Oh God, please don't let me die!" She pleaded in almost inaudible whispers.

Something was wrong. Her face was wet. Something was getting in her eyes. She could hardly breathe now. Her chest ached like when she was little and she and her brother, taking turns with a wristwatch, would count down the seconds to see who could hold their breath the longest. Except then, she could open her mouth wide and suck in deeply as her brother giggled and chided her for not doing better at the contest. Her mouth was open wide now, but nothing was happening. She had almost drowned once, when she was three, and it was like this. Mouth wide, sucking in, no air.

She saw him in the distance, her husband. She noticed the look on his face. He was running, frantic, looking toward her. Confusion was in his eyes. Lips colored white. *Oh God, he's so scared. Don't let me die.* She pleaded again. *Three years. He'll say he was widowed after only three years.*

The sirens could be heard now. People had begun to gather around. She still wasn't sure what had happened, but at the same time, somewhere inside, she knew just what had happened. Had she been here before at some moment in time? It was the oddest sense of confused knowing.

Could you die from pain? she wondered. Maria kept looking around screaming over and over again, "Who did this?"

She heard it then. The voice. The voice behind the metal that had trapped her and tossed her and then discarded her, crumpled, changed forever. She remembered now, watching her get out of the car in a long tan overcoat. She got out a cane and walked slowly, methodically toward the commotion.

"It was me," she said flatly, "I ran over her." The tone. The tone of her voice would haunt her victim for years to come.

Introduction

One morning a few years ago, while I was getting ready for work, the television was tuned in to a news show. An interview with a model was in progress. She had been a survivor of a disaster that had taken place not more than a year earlier. She had suffered pelvic fractures and other injuries similar to mine. She was giving details about her newly published book and saying how she'd learned and grown so much as a person...blah, blah, blah...her voice lost volume as my own inner voice blared. *How could you have learned so much? It's been less than a year!* I felt at that moment like I had been in some kind of remedial recovery program. Was there something I wasn't getting that other trauma survivors got?

The difference, more than anything else, I decided after much thought and, I must admit, some moments of self-deprecation, was her celebrity status in the world. Celebrities are book worthy and their stories of overcoming a trauma sell. The window of opportunity to get their story out is small. I guess that's understandable in a world saturated with the celebrity media. Certainly there was marketability but not believability; at least not to this trauma survivor.

Except for a tiny item in the local newspaper about a pedestrian being hit by a car at the mall, there had been no media attention to the incident. There had been no knocks on my door by a writer with pen cocked, offering to tell my story just days after the ordeal. There had been just me, feeling invisible at times, as I struggled to process all that had happened and integrate all that had changed. I knew that if this had been my experience, then it had more than likely been the experience of many other non-celebrity people in the world. Were there people who perhaps now felt like failures and had lost the lives they once knew because they were still struggling to regain the ground lost by a trauma?

Throughout the years since the accident I've had something nagging at me, telling me to write about my experience. If nothing else, I thought, perhaps I'm just supposed to put it all on paper for *me*. It would be there in black and white, a testimonial of sorts to my spirit, my mind and my precious imperfect, faithful body. Each year that ticked by, I'd chastise myself for not having written my story.

It has taken so long for my story to get written because I had to make sure, before I put it on paper for anyone else's eyes, that I truly believed and lived what I would write. Unlike the survivor example from above, I didn't learn much my first year. I was going from therapy modality to therapy modality, from orthopedist, to physiatrist (physical medicine and rehab doctor), to x-ray, then home. I realize now that the first year was all about getting the basics done. I had to be able to walk without hurting. I had to develop enough stamina to take care of myself, blow-dry my hair, bathe without help, prepare a meal, clean the house, go grocery shopping, and go back to work. Most of the first year was about fixing the body. When I re-read the journal entries I made during that time, it became apparent that my mind was struggling with many things and was treading water in a rough emotional sea as it waited its turn to heal. I am grateful for my spirit, which gave me the strength that encouraged my broken body and soothed my confused mind.

Memories
Chapter One

*Every beginning, after all, is nothing but a sequel,
and the book of events is always open in the middle.*
—Wislawa Szymborska

I pull up to Satellite Coffee in my white Jeep Cherokee. It's not too busy and I'm glad about that, because tonight I will begin the telling of the story. The air is warm for spring, almost summer-like, and the gentle breeze carrying dark clouds from the west is teasing with the possibility of rain. The coffee shop architecture looks both southwestern and space-age. It's located on Montgomery Boulevard, which seems to bustle with traffic no matter the time of day.

The word "Satellite" is neon orange, trimmed in red, written in a font that makes it look like a comet swooshing through the burnished silver rectangle that holds it. The building is brown stucco with red painted rectangular blocks that span its height. Slices of stacked toffee-colored stone permeate the inside of the building's outside boundary. A slender middle-aged man in a white polo and jeans sits outside at the wrought-iron patio table nearest the sleek concrete fountain. Small gusts of wind blow. The steady fall of water from the fountain is interrupted, as it sways to the east with the west wind.

The huge glass door is heavy. I pull hard to open it. The scent of roasted coffee fills my nostrils and the soft jazz, my ears. I order a decaf iced latte and wait under red circular lights imbedded in a silver arch that spans the ceiling. I notice the blue neon backlighting that frames the menus on the wall behind the counter as the young brunette girl in her black Satellite tee shirt hands me the latte and smiles. I look around, wanting to choose just the right spot to delve into memory. The back wall, across from the serving area is a space mural of the universe, giving the raised seating area the feeling of being on the bridge of the Starship Enterprise. I choose a red leather chair rather than one of the tables on the starship bridge. It faces the sliced stone fireplace. There is a 1950s era starburst wall clock above the fireplace opening, its spiked arms alternately colored in turquoise, orange, green, blue and black. The hands on the face read five minutes to eight. I sit down, open a spiral notebook and begin writing.

On my way to the coffee shop I had seen a construction warning sign on the median that flashed hyphenated words in orange lights that read: '6/3-6/5 ... Penn. Cand. inter. ...closed... seek alt. route...' (translation: from 6/3-6/5, the Pennsylvania/Candelaria intersection will be closed, seek alternate route). As I read it I thought that after the accident it would have been handy to have my own (re)construction sign flashing for all who were motoring through my life. Mine would have read: '11/24/97...Alice ... under reconst...seek alt person.' But life isn't like that. Time presses on, scooping us up even when we want it to stand still until we get our bearings back.

In a split second, a life can change. It's both amazing

and dreadful how that can happen. In one instant your life is defined by the known and in the next instant you don't even recognize yourself. It's hard to believe that so many years have passed since the day I was simultaneously tossed about by the undercarriage of a car and the underbelly of my emotions. My concept of safety and well-being skidded to a halt with the screech of the car's tires. Through the first days and weeks I felt as though I was clinging to the slippery wet slope of logic. 'The world was no less safe.' I'd remind myself. 'This was just a fluke. Don't panic.' But I'd slip anyway, centimeter by centimeter. I'd flex my imaginary body and dig my fingers into the muddy earth, and pull myself up groping for something to hang on to, only to slip and lose the small bit of ground I'd gained. I knew deep inside of myself that I had to hang on. I couldn't let myself give in to the free fall of fear.

During the early months of recovery I often searched the bookstores for something written about trauma and how to navigate the healing process. I was discouraged by the lack of help on the subject. There were plenty of books on different aspects of healing from disease or abuse, but none of them dealt specifically with healing from a trauma.

Part of me never wanted to look back on that time as closely as it would take to put my experience on paper. Yet another part of me was never going to leave that place or feel whole until I looked back and stood face to face with it.

I've not had an exemplary life filled with wondrous accomplishments or experiences. I consider myself to be very average. Therefore, I truly believe the successes I have experienced in my recovery are attainable by anyone who may feel lost and frightened at the prospect of their future after a traumatic accident. The journey of writing this book put me face to face with the long path traveled. Hopefully my story will help another glean insight about their purpose and place in a world that chose to spare their life.

I was a scrawny little girl. Stick legs and always two sizes smaller than other girls the same age. My dad was career navy and we traveled from duty station to duty station throughout my childhood. I attended seven schools in nine years and had adapting to change down to a science.

My brother and I were close growing up. The familiarity of each other was our comfort until we made new friends and started life over at yet another duty station. I was the stereotypical responsible eldest child. I took quick charge of my baby sister born three months shy of my eleventh birthday. I don't know how I actually was as a child, but I know I always felt older and more responsible than my years. I did everything too young. I was married at eighteen, a mother at twenty, divorced by twenty-two, remarried and a mother again at twenty-three.

My twenties were all about struggling to make the scattered pieces of the life I'd created fit together somehow to form what I wanted me to be. Nothing came easy. My first son, Brandon, was born on Oahu. The free-spirited beach baby, born to a twenty-year-old hippie, a "Take your baby to Diamond Head Crater for an all-day concert" kind of mom. My second son, Aaron, was born in a Michigan birthing center the day after the New Year. The snow baby who was brought home just ten short hours after his birth by his twenty-three-year-old, born-again Christian mom who just knew that she had found the answers to all that life had to offer. But fifteen years and a second divorce later I found myself starting over in a small South Georgia town with two teenage sons, in an apartment for low-income tenants, with a retail job that paid seven dollars an hour. I guess the collective 'church' had not agreed with my choice to divorce (though no one dared come right out and say so), for I was quietly dropped by every friend I'd had for the last ten years, with the exception of Susan, who is still my dearest friend and most staunch supporter.

One thing's for sure, life goes on, even when all we think we know is not exactly as we thought. I married again. Barry is calm and steady. And I truly don't know what I would have done without him all these years. He kept me solidly in his care through one of the most difficult times in my life.

On November 24, 1997 I went into work early because we had a floor move to do in the store where I was an assistant manager. We always went in early (usually myself and the manager) in order to re-merchandise and freshen up the displays before sales or changes in seasons. This was our usual Christmas kick-off/pre-Thanksgiving floor move. The early morning November air was as it always is in Albuquerque, crisp and fresh. I had parked near our employee entrance and had gone back to the parking lot close to opening time in order to move my car to the designated employee parking area. I was walking from my parked car to the mall employee entrance when I was bumped from behind by a large object. At first, I had no idea what bumped me. I instinctively put my hand behind me, touched metal and had begun to turn when I was bumped again even harder, as the object I now knew was a car, sped up. I was immediately struck down between the front tires, and the fight for my life began.

I remember every moment, in slow motion. With the impact of the now speeding car, I crumpled between the front tires as my legs were knocked out from under me. My left foot was run over by the driver's side tire and I began tumbling and hitting the undercarriage of the car as it careened over me. I tried to move myself in those seconds, so that the car would pass over me without running over me again, but my body wasn't cooperating with my mind. During one of the many tumbles under the car, my head was facing the rear passenger tire and I saw it coming straight for my neck. I frantically tried to lunge out from under the car. I succeeded in sparing my head and neck, with the tire running over my left back and shoulder. The impact rolled me over again and thrust me out the rear of the car. As I lay there I saw the car drive away. It was stopped by mall employees that had witnessed the accident. My body began to frantically try to get up. As I tried to set my hands on the pavement my legs, damaged by the impact, splayed under the weight of my body. I remembered a deer I had seen once on a Georgia road. It had been struck by a car and it was struggling to regain its footing. I remembered seeing its eyes and the panic I saw in them. I wondered if my eyes looked like the deer's eyes I had seen that day. Again and again, compelled by some unseen force, I tried to stand. Then I felt someone's hand on my back and heard a man's voice say, "Stay down. Stay down!" just as my legs and arms collapsed to the pavement once again.

He began to ask me questions. "Who are you? Do you work in the mall?" I rattled off information as fast as I could, thinking I had to talk fast for I was surely going to die. My heart was racing and it was getting hard to breathe. He didn't leave me, but instructed another bystander to go into the store where I worked and tell someone named Maria what had happened.

I heard him say, "She wants Maria to call her husband. They live close by."

He continued to tell me I would be all right. I could feel his hand on my back. "Just be still, you'll be OK," he said over and over. I know that only minutes passed, though it felt like I had been thrust into a strange world where clocks ticked in slow motion as you experienced life in someone else's body.

I could see Maria running toward me now. She crouched down beside me and said I'd be fine. She began stroking my head. I was afraid that I was dying. I could only take small shallow breaths and the pain was so unbearable. I could feel something wet trickling down my face. A crowd was gathering. Maria kept asking everyone if they knew who did this. I don't know if anyone replied. I was asking Maria If I was dying. She said that I wasn't. I remember seeing her tears and wondered if she knew I wouldn't make it.

"I can't breathe, Maria. It hurts. I'm going to die. Am I going to die? Maria, am I going to die?" I whispered over and over, almost breathless with the effort.

"You're not going to die. You just hang in there. You're going to be OK," she said as her eyes darted from me to the crowd and then back to me again. Just then, as Maria screamed at the now gathering crowd again, "Who did this?"

I saw her. She was an elderly, gray-haired woman getting out of her car. She moved slowly as she got out. The employees who had stopped the car were all around her as though they expected her to bolt. She reached into the back seat and retrieved a cane, then began walking toward me. *It was her! She hit me! Why? Do I know her?* My mind raced with questions. *How did this happen? Was it on purpose? Why did this woman who I don't recognize do this to me?*

Even in the surreal place between lucidity and shock, my eyes were fixed on the face of this stranger as my mind searched its memory banks to try to match the puzzle pieces and come up with an image that made sense.

"You're doing fine. The ambulance is on its way. I called Barry. Who the hell did this? Where is the damn person who was driving the car?" Maria yelled, looking around.

"I am. I ran over her." She said as she approached my body. She just stood there. I could see the bottom of her tan overcoat, the worn rubber tip of her wooden cane and her stockinged legs. She was quiet. No crying, no panic. No words of apology. No asking if I was all right, nothing. She just stood there looking down at me.

Just then, I saw Barry running across the parking lot. He looked toward me and I wondered if that would be the last time I would see him. My nostrils were flooded with the memory of his scent. My eyes stung at the sight of him. Without warning I began panicking about my children. My sons were seventeen and twenty. *I can't die! I have to see my sons! I'm not finished raising them! What would happen to my family?* I could hear the sirens now. I was relieved because I had stayed alive long enough for help to arrive. This was the first of many hurdles I'd have to conquer.

The paramedics arrived and began working on me. The police and mandatory fire truck were now there as well. I was immobilized on the backboard and in excruciating pain. I couldn't catch my breath. The paramedics kept asking me questions as one of them palpated my body for injuries and others unloaded their gear. I just kept saying over and over that my leg hurt and I couldn't breathe. Barry was talking to someone. The trench coat was gone. Maria was gone. I could only hear commotion. Barry's voice faded into the background. I felt confused. I was breathing so shallowly now. Someone was explaining everything that was being done to me. I was being lifted into the waiting ambulance. My right leg, my back, between my legs and my chest hurt fiercely. Inside the ambulance they began cutting of my clothes. I fought the oxygen mask. I felt like I was being smothered. I was told to relax. I closed my eyes. I was tired now and too exhausted to fight anymore.

Journal entry: October 22, 1997

Reflection: Friend or Foe? I know now that it depends only on your frame of mind. At one time you can reflect on a situation in your life and see the negative, at another point in time you'll see the same incident in a positive way. How unusual "frame of mind" is.

Change

Chapter Two

Change, when it comes, cracks everything open.
—Dorothy Allison

    I don't have many memories from my experience in triage. I know that my right hip was dislocated and that it had to be reduced (put back in its socket) quickly. I got scolded by a nurse with a British accent for pinching people through the bars of the gurney. Someone was scrubbing the gash on my stomach and it hurt so badly, that I pinched whatever was in my reach. Someone else was putting tubes down my nose. I was thrashing about, crying out, and apparently, pinching people in sensitive places.

    I also remember only bits and pieces from the visits in ICU. I remember feeling so disconnected with what had happened. I would fade in and out of that place of knowing what had happened and confusion about what had happened. I couldn't comprehend whether I had died or was still living. I was on a morphine drip. My toes would wiggle, but I couldn't move my legs.

    I was on the backboard for two of the three days I was in ICU in order for the results from the CT scans of my cervical spine to be confirmed negative for fractures. I did have several broken ribs, a broken ankle (which wasn't diagnosed and cast until three weeks later), several pelvic fractures, a fractured scapula and clavicle (compliments of the rear tire I tried to avoid), a plethora of cuts, gashes and soft tissue injuries. The skin between my eyes had been ripped and there was a nasty jagged cut that ran almost the length of my scalp. It required stitching twice because it was done improperly the first time. I had been losing blood and was fading in and out of consciousness. Because of this stitching error, I had to have three units of blood.

I do remember calling out one time, to the shadows walking back and forth on the other side of the sliding glass door to my room.

"Hello? Hello? Hello, is anyone there?" I called out in whispers.

A nurse heard me and came into my room. "Hi honey. Is everything all right?" She asked, touching my arm.

"Where am I? Am I dead?" I asked.

"No hon, you're in the intensive care unit. Do you remember getting in an accident?"

"I think I got run over by a car. Is that what happened?"

"You did. You're doing great, though. Here's the buzzer. If you need me, you press it," I nodded and she left.

On the third day in ICU, I began to smell an awful odor near me. A kind male technician who really should have been moonlighting at a comedy club was in my room doing 'tech' things, and I remember asking him what the bad odor was.

"Oh, sweetie," he replied, "That's you."

"What do you mean, that's me?"

"It's your hair," he said touching the blood encrusted, top of my head. "There's a lot of blood in there and well, blood's a living organism and well, it's decomposing."

"Oh my God! Can you wash my hair? I mean are you allowed to do that? I smell so bad!"

"I think I can help out with that." He said. "You wait right here," he said, winking. "I'll be right back."

After a few minutes he reappeared, carrying towels, a basin and several bottles of peroxide. He set up his workstation at the head of my bed and began pouring the peroxide over my hair. The fizzing of the peroxide tickled and made my head itch. I could not believe how good the cool liquid felt on my head, but unfortunately for anyone equipped with a nose, the smell that was emanating from my hair became even worse. As the clumps of blood began to loosen, he gently massaged the foamy mess with his gloved hands.

"Oh my! Oh my!" he'd say periodically, as he pulled away ponytail chunks of hair that had glued themselves to my scalp, but were no longer attached. It was gross, and took a long time, but I must say I felt much better.

"Your spa treatment is over, Mrs. Hurst," He said. "If you could wash your hair between visits it would be greatly appreciated by the technician."

"I'll make sure to do that!" I smiled.

My eldest son, Brandon, drove from Utah when he heard the news of the accident. He had already made plans to spend Thanksgiving with us and this had brought him home sooner. My sister Patti and her four-year-old son flew in from Phoenix. The fear I saw in my sister's tearful eyes the first time she saw me set my determination to recover. I could tell by her expression that my face probably looked bad. Days later, I would ask her for a mirror and gasp at the stranger looking at me.

I remember Barry constantly telling me that everything would be OK. I remember that my mom rarely left my side and became a warrior. Her insistence that something was wrong with me during the time that I was bleeding internally from the incomplete suturing of my head wound more than likely saved my life. Aaron, my 17-year-old son, would hold my hand and with a trembling smile ask me if I was all right.

On Thanksgiving Day my condition was upgraded and I was transferred out of ICU to the orthopedic ward. Gratefulness comes in all sizes. Now the mental and physical battle with my fate would begin. The physical transfer was excruciating. Four people on either side of my gurney lifted the sheet simultaneously on the count of three and swung me onto the bed.

My family came to visit and Mom brought me a plate from their Thanksgiving dinner. I took a few bites, mostly to reassure everyone. I think it made them feel better to see that I could eat. I spent the rest of the evening talking with Brandon about his life in Utah, and with my sister about what was going on in Phoenix, where she lived. I seemed to thirst for normalcy, thinking that somehow this would make the surreal place where I found myself magically vaporize. Everyone stayed until visiting hours were over and I was left alone with myself, off the morphine that had kept me from thinking clearly, and I was beginning to feel the pangs of panic.

I lie there in my bed, grasping for anything in my arsenal of life that could keep me from feeling like I was going to die from fear. I knew that I wasn't paralyzed because I had wiggled my toes at every opportunity since

I had broken free from the car's undercarriage. But I was frightened about what was going to happen to me now. There was probably not one inch of me that didn't hurt. I couldn't move to reposition myself, so I lay there alone and began to sob. I cried silently until I had drained myself of any remaining energy. Why hadn't I died? It seemed that all I had ever done in my life was to make mistakes, so why was I spared? I felt guilty for being alive. I felt relieved because I was alive.

I took a deep breath and realized that this was now my reality and, like it or not, it was the journey I was on. I had no more tears and lay there in the dark, still and alone. I began to inspect my body with timid touches. I glided shaky, asphalt-scraped fingers over my arms and felt for each cut. My hands gingerly skimmed over the dinner-plate-size bruises that covered my hips and thighs, I winced with each light stroke. I touched the sharp bump at my shoulder that was the result of the broken clavicle. My hand quickly jerked away as it felt the deformity from the fractured, misaligned bone. A single hot tear made its way down my cheek as I took a deep breath and gently tapped at the gash between my eyes, following the jagged path of torn skin. I placed my fingers in my hair, finding the scalp and tracing the path of the railroad tie staples. I stroked the prickly shaved hair that was already growing back. I worried about how much of my hair was missing, and immediately felt the vanity of the thought. I searched for the gash on my stomach, lifted my gown and squinted to see it in the dark. My arms and legs were mine fields of cuts and bruises. The nail on my right pinky finger was ripped off past the quick and my chest was a mass of bruises. The inside of my left calf had been branded by a grid pattern from the car's undercarriage and there were tread marks on my arms. I still had oxygen flowing through a nose tube. My breathing was shallow from the swollen tissue around the rib fractures.

I closed my eyes and touched each of those places again. As warm tears puddled on my neck, I whispered to my body that we would heal. I imagined my blood coursing through the damaged tissue, bringing life-sustaining nourishment. I visualized my bones growing back together, healing. I whispered reassuring words to my body as though it was an entity separate from me that was hurting and needed care.

"All right," I softly spoke to my mind and body, "We have to pull together. We only have two choices, give up or fight."

That was the beginning of my daily ritual. Whenever I was alone I would close my eyes and visualize my body healing from the tiniest cell to the largest bone. I would stroke my left foot with my right foot (my left ankle wouldn't move) and touch each broken, bruised, or cut part, encouraging them to heal. If I couldn't actually touch the injured part, I would imagine touching it. I would take deep breaths and tell myself that everything was going to be fine. I was determined to recover. It was the only choice as I saw it.

During this time, I imagined two scenarios. I chose five years down the road, two paths. I imagined people who knew me today, five years into the future. The one scenario had me beaten by this traumatic experience. I would imagine people saying, "Whatever happened to Alice? You remember. She was run over at the mall? It's so sad. She lost everything. She still can't walk very well on her own. She lost her job. She was so overwhelmed with self-pity and became so hard to live with that her husband, poor thing, ended up leaving her. Her sons and family aren't even the same anymore. It makes you so fearful that something bad like that could happen to you."

The second scenario had me traveling down a different path. I would imagine people saying, "That's Alice. Did you know she was run over by a car five years ago? I can hardly believe it! You wouldn't know something like that had happened to her unless she told you. I tell you what, she is really a fighter. She was simply walking into work when it happened. You just never know."

I chose scenario number two. I didn't want my life to be defined by this incident. I made my mind up at that moment that I was going to fight every inch of the way to ensure a good turnout.

On day number five I was told that I would start physical therapy. A tech came into my room with a wheelchair and a transfer board. Just sitting me up at an angle close to 45 degrees caused tremendous pain. My unstable, fractured pelvis shifted and made a clicking noise with every movement. I took a deep breath and looked at the properly placed board.

Nope. There was no way I could breathe away the pain of trying to scoot my fractured pelvis across that board! I thought. My husband then decided that he'd lift me to a standing position and we'd move the six inches to the waiting wheelchair. I put my one "good" arm around his neck as he lifted me up. I was standing, dizzy, weak, and shaking. Barry then told me to move one foot at a time toward the chair. My feet went nowhere. They wouldn't do what my mind was willing them to do! I panicked.

"Barry, I can't. My legs won't move! Oh God, what's wrong?" I began to tear up, burying my head in his shoulder, soothing myself with the scent of him, wanting so badly for this not to be my new reality.

"Just relax, everything's OK." He reassured me.

"Barry, are the doctors keeping something from me?"

"They're not keeping anything from you. Just relax and I'll help move you to the wheelchair." He then guided my broken body to the wheelchair and I was shuttled to the physical therapy unit of the hospital.

Any illusions of being able to bounce right back from this were now gone. This was a huge letdown for me. I got scared about my future again. The therapy session was painful and only revealed how injured I was. Other than getting vertical while being helped from the hospital bed to the wheelchair, I accomplished nothing at physical therapy. I felt as though my body no longer belonged to me. My legs didn't move when my mind said, *move*. It was as though they had forgotten what they used to do automatically. We were strangers, unable to communicate with each other.

When back in bed, I'd begin speaking to my body. I envisioned each muscle and would try to contract it when my mind concentrated on it. I decided that I would do my best to nourish my body with food and encouraging words and work hard in physical therapy once I could move better.

Sometimes while alone, I would go over that day again and again in my mind. The 'What ifs' haunted me. If only I hadn't had to move my car from one parking area to another, but I did. If only the driver hadn't panicked and hit the gas instead of the brake, I probably would have gotten away with just cuts and bruises, but she didn't. If I hadn't been wearing a bulky sweater, I might not have gotten hung up in the undercarriage and could have avoided the back tire running over me, but I had. These thoughts would tumble over and over in my mind. I would feel angry that this elderly lady, who just four months earlier had gotten her license renewed, was driving in the first place. I was angry that she hit the gas instead of the brake, which threw me to the ground. I was mad I had worn a stupid bulky sweater that day, and that during the holiday season mall employees had to park so far away from the entrance. But always after the negative 'what ifs,' came the positive 'what ifs.' What if I had lost consciousness one of the times my head hit the pavement, but I didn't. What if I hadn't seen that ominous back tire coming toward my head, but I did. And what if I hadn't been able to move those few inches that spared my skull or neck from being fractured, but I had.

I couldn't figure out *why* this had happened to me. I realize that there are many people who believe that there are reasons *why* accidents or illnesses happen. The usual platitudes are given with somber, knowing looks and somehow that is supposed to make it all better. All the "There must have been a good reason" and the "God knew you could handle this" statements; along with the admonishments to feel *lucky* and *grateful* that you came out of it as well as you did, really didn't make me feel a bit better about my circumstance. In actuality they don't do much to placate me even now.

"Your angels were certainly watching over you!" some unfortunate soul said to me one day while in the hospital.

"You're kidding, right?" I retorted, "My angels were NOT watching over me or else they would have seen what was about to happen and kept the car off me in the first place. Who needs angels that aren't even paying attention?" I watched as the knowing smile on the stranger's face faded.

"Ahem," she cleared her throat, "I hope you do well."

"Yeah, thanks" I replied.

Because I probably wasn't going to suffer permanent disability, I was supposed to feel *lucky*. Well I didn't. I felt victimized. I was in the most pain I'd ever experienced and I was angry. I didn't know how much of what had happened to my body would be permanent. Feeling *lucky* was not in my repertoire of emotions right then. Temporary disability is still disability. It still requires effort to overcome and in many cases will leave permanent residual effects that have to be accepted for the rest of one's life. I would be grateful for many things that came from this experience. But they would come later, in time, once I could come to some resolution about my situation. Being expected to respond well to the idea of gratefulness so soon after the impact of this random injustice of life was an unfair expectation. The one thing I could do for myself right now, in order to cope, was not to reflect on *"Why"* but rather on *"What now?"* What do I do now that this has happened to me? I either give in to fear, frustration, worry, self-pity, and the physical weakness I feel in my body, or fight. I fight to be positive and to get my body functional again.

On the sixth day, the doctor asked if I'd like to go home the following day. Of course I'd love to go home! But as the day wore on I began to worry about my ability to go home. I was still using a bedpan. I couldn't sit up without the triangle apparatus that hung over my bed. I couldn't stand or take a step. I had no way of getting around if I did go home. The pain was almost unbearable, even with strong pain medication. I told the physical therapist that day that the doctor had said that I could go home, but now I didn't know how that could be done. I was upset and began to cry. Later that day, a nurse came in and said that the doctor would like to know if I felt like I could go home. I assumed that the therapist had reported my emotional conversation with her. I told the nurse that I didn't see how I could. I was given a reprieve of sorts. I could stay a couple more days.

As usual, the night nurse came in to my room about midnight to check vitals. She would always chat with me for a few minutes. She must have sensed that something was wrong because she asked me if I was all right. Over the years I had built a nice sturdy wall around my soft inner self and wasn't known for crying much. But since this incident, I had turned into a weepy mess. It was irritating to me. Through the frustrating tears that I could no longer control, I relayed the day's events with the doctor and about going home. I told her that I really wanted to go home, but how could I in this state? There was no way I could manage. My husband worked nights and we couldn't afford for him to take any more time off. My son went to school during the day and worked at night. My mother needed to stay home because my father had multiple sclerosis and was bedridden. I couldn't ambulate at all at this point. I didn't know what I was going to do. I had one more day of therapy and then they were going to kick me to the proverbial curb. She told me that they certainly couldn't make me leave, but that I would recover much better in a rehabilitation hospital. I didn't know that a rehabilitation hospital was an option. I'd heard of professional athletes going to rehabilitation hospitals but I didn't know that they were for just anyone. I began to allow myself to feel excited. She explained more about what rehab hospitals were and I began to feel better. She mentioned the names of two that were in our city and by the next evening my husband had gotten the ball moving.

This recovery process was going to be a series of highs and lows. Each hopeful or successful moment seemed to be followed by a disappointment. I was determined to learn to appreciate my small successes and joyful moments.

Rehab
CHAPTER THREE

Life is not easy for any of us, but what of that?
We must have perseverance and ... confidence in ourselves.
—Marie Curie

It was Monday, December 2, 1997. There were snow flurries outside. Today was the big day! I was being discharged from the university hospital to the rehab hospital. It seemed as though the accident had happened so long ago, yet it had only been eight days. I still couldn't fully comprehend that this had happened to me. Now that the initial shock of getting run over had subsided, I had to get better. I sure as hell wasn't going to spend the rest of my life whimpering in a corner. I mean, I'd fought the underbelly of a car and won! To see me you wouldn't have thought I'd been the victor, but I was and would continue to be. The event itself was none of my doing, but the recovery would be all of my doing. I set my jaw in determination, pulled myself up on my bed using the triangle that was hanging overhead and craned my neck to see the world outside my fourth-story window. The world that I would soon rejoin.

A representative for the rehabilitation hospital came into my room and began telling me and my husband about my stay there. I was asked about my goals for recovery. The representative was upbeat and had such faith in my ability to recover that by the time the paramedics came into my room to transport me by ambulance to my new accommodations, I was feeling excited and eager for this new adventure to begin. The transfer from hospital bed to gurney was never a pleasant experience. I would be lifted, sheet and all to the waiting gurney. I couldn't be rolled over due to the pelvic fractures. The whole process would always make me cringe because of the pain involved and that creepy sensation of bone shifting inside the skin.

As the doors to the outside were opened, I was embraced by the crisp, cold, winter air around me. Snowflakes landed softly on my face like little wet kisses from the heavens.

"Could you walk slowly?" I asked the female paramedic pushing the gurney. "I haven't been outside in what seems like forever and it feels so good."

She smiled, "Sure. I think we can do that." She slowed her pace and we strolled to the waiting transport vehicle.

There were no sirens this time. No rushed movements, just me, the male paramedic who was driving, and the female paramedic sitting in the back with me.

We arrived without incident and I was wheeled into my new room. I had a roommate. It looked as though she also had just arrived. She and I exchanged silent glances. The room was huge compared to the room I'd had at the university hospital. Everything was handicap accessible. The paramedics wheeled me in, transferred me to my bed and wished me luck. I looked around, taking in the pale blue walls, the writing desk built into the wall with an extra wide space under it to accommodate a wheelchair, the entrance to the bathroom with its wide door and the large low window to the left of my bed. I closed my eyes, took a deep breath and settled into the rehab phase of this ordeal.

So many changes happened that first day. Barry saw to it that I was settled in and stayed as long as he could before he left for work. The hospital was close to his workplace, so he said he'd come by later to see how I was doing. A physician and a nurse came by to do a check-in exam. The dietician went over my meal plan. But the *pièce de résistance* of my check-in process was the interview I had with this young aide dressed in scrubs. The scrub top was floral with ruffles around the sleeves and bottom hem. There was a tie at the waist that was done in a little bow at the back. She reminded me of Minnie Mouse and I smiled. She began asking me questions about the symptoms I'd been experiencing since the accident, and with each answer she colored in little boxes that reflected my answers.

"Have you had a loss of appetite?" she asked. "How long has it been since you had a bowel movement? Have you urinated on your own since having the catheter removed?" And so on. I remember in particular one question that I thought so absurd it was funny. As she made her way down the page she looked at me inquisitively and said, with a straight face, "Would you say you've been depressed since the accident?"

I thought, *you're not serious, right? Hmmm, would it be unusual if I answered yes? Why should I be depressed? In the blink of an eye my whole world changed. Twelve fractures, a dislocated hip, covered in cuts and bruises, bald spots on my head, I can't stand, roll over, sit up or take care of my most private needs and you truly want an answer to that question?*

"Yes, I have." I answered.

"Mildly or very?" she pressed.

See. I couldn't have asked me that question, had I been in her place. I would have definitely skipped that one. I mused.

"Very." I replied.

The young aide left and suddenly my roommate began to laugh. Her name was Carol. This became a standing joke between us during our stay. We'd ask each other sometimes, "Have you been depressed since the accident?" Wait for the answer, then follow with, "Mildly or very?" and then we'd hoot wildly (which was excruciatingly painful, I might add).

It was still my first day and I had told Minnie Mouse, when she asked if there was anything she could get for me that would be helpful to me during my stay, that at the other hospital I had a triangle apparatus hanging over my bed that helped me when I was trying to sit up. She said that she would see what she could do. A couple of hours later, I watched as a man took the triangle unit out of its box and began attaching it to the head of my bed.

A short, stout woman with blonde, spiked hair, who looked to be in her thirties, came into the room carrying a clipboard. "Excuse me!" she said forcefully, startling both me and the man setting up the triangle. "May I ask what you are doing?"

"I'm setting up the triangle that was requisitioned for this patient." He said. Composure regained, he turned to his work.

"No! This won't be needed. Take it down." She ordered.

"I asked for it." I interjected. "I had one at the other hospital and it was very helpful"

"I'm sure it was, but you won't be using it here. Go

ahead and take it away." She instructed again, waving her hand in the direction of the partially assembled triangle. The man began to take the triangle apart.

"I can't sit up without it." I said, almost in tears.

"You'll learn. That thing will only make you lazy." And with that she turned to me with her brightest smile and an outstretched hand, "Hi! I'm Sue, your physical therapist."

She wasn't much on charm, but she was good at what she did. Over the next two weeks she had me progressing at lightning speed. I had a schedule that was more like boot camp than a hospital stay. There were sheet changes from 7:00 to 7:30. Breakfast was served in our rooms from 7:30 to 8:00. (This was the only meal allowed in-room. All other meals had to be taken in the cafeteria unless you had special needs or permission from your doctor.) From 9:00 to 9:30 was upper extremity class, then a break. At 10:00 it was back to the gym again for another class. Usually lower extremity exercises, pool therapy or manual therapy with ultrasound or iontophoresis. (This is a technique using a small electric charge to deliver a medicine or other chemical through the skin. It's basically an injection without the needle.) Then I'd wheel myself back to my room in the huge reclining wheelchair used when hip precautions (which meant I was not yet allowed to sit at a 90° angle) were necessary. It was heavy and was hard to maneuver.

Medication would be dispensed and I'd take a nap before lunch. Usually there would be a visit from the occupational therapist, who was in charge of retraining me to do daily-living tasks. The tasks were exhausting and required all sorts of gadgets to help me do things my uninjured body used to do without a second thought. Lunch would be served at noon. Barry would usually come and eat lunch with me before he went to work. There would be more therapy throughout the afternoon, then dinner, and off to bed, exhausted. Each day would pass much like the previous one. As improvement was achieved, new tasks would be added.

Carol had arrived on the same day I did, but about an hour earlier. She was in her fifties, had tripped over her purse strap while at work and fractured her hip. She found out at the hospital that she had osteoporosis, had shattered her hip and had to have emergency hip replacement surgery. We became fast friends and almost inseparable during our stay.

We had each been given the helpful "claw" device. It was a grabber that we could use to reach for things without bending. We both had hip precautions and weren't allowed to bend—not that we could, mind you.

One night, Carol's claw dropped off her bed. She whispered, "Alice."

"Yeah?" I replied.

"I dropped my claw. Do you think you could reach it with your claw and hand it to me?"

So here we were, both reaching between our beds, as far as we dared, not wanting to fall out of the damn things, for the fugitive claw. We began giggling and groaning so much that we had to take a break from our claw retrieval expedition in order to recuperate. This unfortunate incident repeated itself days later when my claw dropped from my bed. We got along well. We would encourage each other and I felt grateful for her presence and her sense of humor.

I saw so many severely injured people. There were

those who had suffered strokes, gunshot wounds and falls that had left them paraplegic or quadriplegic. Some had brain injuries from various tragedies. It was moving to see the struggles others had to endure.

In the room next to mine was a man in his thirties who had also been run over by a car. An elderly man had hit the gas rather than the brake upon impact, just like what had happened to me. This young man had not fared as well as I. He was now facing life as a quadriplegic. *Why did I get away with this?* I wondered. *Why am I going to walk again and he's not?* I didn't feel worthy of my good fortune. I have thought about him often since then and always whisper a prayer on his behalf.

Carol left the hospital the following week. I wished her well, and we promised to stay in touch. I was going to miss her. My replacement roommate was not at all like Carol. She was an eighty-something-year-old woman to whom I took an immediate dislike. I knew it was because she reminded me of the woman who had run over me. I avoided her as much as possible, and during one of my visits with the psychologist, became tearful while expressing my dislike for this woman. The psychologist assured me that my emotions were normal and that as time passed I would feel differently. Still, I could barely stand to look at her. I stayed out of my room much of each day. Saturday, December 7th was going to be my first day pass and it couldn't have come at a better time. I needed to get away.

Journal Entry: Saturday, December 7, 1997

"I was able to leave the rehab hospital today for a home visit. I

was given my dose of medication before I left, because they won't let me take any medication with me. I have an eight-hour pass. Barry came for me in his truck because I can't bend enough to get into the Cavalier. I have a walker now. I have been practicing walking with it over all types of terrain all week with my physical therapist. She wanted to know about my home. How many steps were there? What kind of surfaces would I be walking on, etc? As soon as I was in the truck on my way home, I began to cry. My life has changed so much. Will it ever be the same? Hopefully I'll be released next Monday, Barry's birthday. I have to see if Maria will shop for Barry's birthday gift. This really sucks!

It was so wonderful to be inside my own house! The scent of it; familiar surroundings that now seem almost foreign. I tried to remove a load of laundry from the washer and put it in the dryer and was so weak that I had to call Barry to help. I cried because of the reality of my weakness. We ordered a pizza and watched T.V. As much as I hated it, I had to take a nap. My body is still so foreign to me! I stayed home till about 5:00 p.m. The medication had worn off and I needed to go back. On the way to the hospital, I cried again. This was so sad for me. I'm so angry that this has happened to me. I don't know how I'm ever going to be normal again. This has been one of those days when I feel like I can't do this. It's too much for me to handle.

I was expecting to be discharged in a week, so I spent the last few days of my hospitalization preparing to go home. The occupational therapist spent the last days teaching me techniques to help with the tasks I'd have to do when I got home. I had to force myself to put on makeup and blow-dry my hair, which just exhausted me. It took me twice as long as it should have. I began to feel sadness creeping over me as I tried to deal with all this. The physical therapy had helped me, but I was so frustrated with what seemed like minimal achievements now. Maybe my expectations were too high, or maybe I had just become used to the leaps-and-bounds type of progress I had initially enjoyed. I mean, I hadn't been able to even get out of bed unaided just two short weeks earlier.

I remember the first time (on day two of my stay in the rehab hospital) my therapist stood me up between the parallel bars and I took my first steps. My hands felt clammy and I was shaking. I strained to hold up my body as she rolled herself backward on a stool in front of me while a physical therapy technician followed behind with the wheelchair. My pelvis made a clicking noise with any movement and felt like it was shifting inside me with every step. Before I had walked the length of the bars, I was exhausted. And now I was cruising around the hospital in my chair, and even going outside into the courtyard sometimes. I would use my walker for gait training and the wheelchair for trips to physical therapy or the pool. I would fold up the walker and transport it on my lap as I wheeled to my destination, feeling quite free and accomplished as I managed my temporary wheels. Using the walker still tired me. It was hard for me to keep the fear away. I knew I had progressed well, but still, here I was in a wheelchair two weeks before Christmas. I was such a different person from what I had been just three short weeks before.

One evening I was returning from the isolated cafeteria with a snack I had procured and was rolling my chair down the empty hallway. It was dark outside and the windows reflected the inside like a mirror. As I looked out the large glass windows that spanned the length of the corridor, I caught my reflection in the glass. It seemed as though I was looking at someone else. There I was dressed in my latest fashion trend, the wind suit, rolling in my chair. Suddenly without warning the tears began to flow. I took a deep breath and one last look as I rolled away.

As the time to be released drew near, just days now, I felt the pressure of returning to realm of the normal. I was terrified. The day had finally come, December 16, 1997, Barry's birthday. My discharge team met that morning to discuss my progress. They met with Barry, filling him in on the details of my care and then signed the release. My bag was packed. I was sitting on the edge of my bed looking out the window into the courtyard that had kept me company during all those lonely moonlit nights. All my new tools for daily living were neatly stowed away. I had my claw, the sock puller-upper thingy, my walker, and all my hospital 'souvenirs.' My left foot was still hard as a rock, and I was kind of worried about it. I had an appointment at the university hospital in just an hour and I was going to see if I could get it x-rayed. The resident doctor at the rehab hospital didn't seem to think it was anything more than soft tissue injury, but it hadn't seen the progress the other soft tissue injuries had seen.

Barry came to my room and gathered up my stuff. As I walked down the hallway for the last time, I glanced into all the familiar rooms filled with the strangers that had become such familiar faces to me.

There was the thirty-something young man in the room next door who had also gotten run over by an elderly driver. He was struggling with the difficulties of quadriplegia. I smiled meekly at him as I glanced his way and breathed a prayer of success for his recovery.

I saw the young teenage guy who had been in some

of my "Macarena therapy sessions" (you don't want to know!) recovering from a gunshot wound to his head. Had he learned his lesson, I wondered, or would he go back to the gang lifestyle that had almost taken his life?

Toward the end of the corridor there was the little, elderly, Native American lady who had reminded me so much of my grandmother Ramoncita, her room filled with family, recovering from a stroke the best she could at eighty-something.

She was "Gramita" to another funny Hispanic man in our therapy circle. He would cheer her on during our balloon-batting upper extremity therapy.

"Come on Gramita, you can do it!" he'd cheer. "Hit it! That's good, Gramita, way to go!" We'd all laugh at his antics, as would Gramita.

The last room before freedom was the one with the retired gentleman, though gentle man he was not, who refused to do most of what the therapist asked during his sessions. He had experienced a mild stroke. Sometimes I'd watch him from my mat table, which was set up next to his. I'd listen as he complained and cussed with each instruction from the therapist. He was angry and had probably always been less than delightful. His wife was there every day, never seeming to take notice of his gruff manner. She came to the door as I passed by with my husband and belongings in tow.

"You going home today honey?" she asked.

"Finally," I replied.

"I'll surely miss your smile. You have the best outlook. Take care of yourself and get well," she encouraged.

"I will," I promised. "Good luck to you as well."

"Thanks, dear. I'll need it, won't I?" She winked as she

motioned with her head toward her husband, who was on his bed drinking something through a straw.

I have the best outlook? That's what she said. I wasn't so sure I agreed.

I had the usual four-hour wait to see the orthopedist at the university hospital. It was almost unbearable. I felt weak and nauseous as we waited to see the doctor. Everything hurt and I could hardly wait to get home and go to bed. I requested an x-ray of my foot. The orthopedist examined me and agreed. I made my way with the walker to radiology. While waiting, the receptionist and I began to talk. She asked what had happened to me. I told her. After I had the x-rays and was leaving she said,

"In a year, you'll be so much better."

I smiled politely and responded, "I hope you're right," not at all believing her.

It was discovered that I did indeed have a fracture, and it was one that would more than likely need surgical intervention. The orthopedist wanted to readmit me and place pins in my ankle. My eyes welled with tears. I asked if I had a choice. The crack on my ankle didn't seem that bad as I looked at the illuminated images.

"Can't I just have it cast?" I asked. He looked at the films of my ankle again, marking the visible fracture with a Sharpie.

"Surgery will be better for you in the long run." he said. "You could have problems with this ankle forever." He warned, eyes peering over his glasses.

In the end he reluctantly agreed to let me have a cast, but I could tell that he had his reservations about this. I thanked him and apologized for being upset, but I really couldn't imagine being readmitted, much less undergoing surgery and having to 'start over' in many ways. He said he understood and I was escorted into the casting area.

I entered my home with the cast on my left leg up to my knee, maneuvering the walker up the step to the entrance. My pelvis was hurting as it shifted, bearing the new weight. Both shoulders were burning and all I could think about was lying down. Barry had spent his birthday in hospitals. I was hurting, tired, and was feeling a bit guilty for being such a burden on his special day. Barry didn't seem to mind, though, and helped me into bed, covered me like a child, and I slept. It was surreal, being home. I felt lost in my most familiar environment.

Christmas came and went. I tired easily and even the holiday excitement couldn't keep me from having to nap. I've always hated naps. I would be so glad when my body could function for a whole day. We had a quiet holiday. I had actually bought and wrapped all the gifts before Thanksgiving this year for the first time ever. It was almost as though something knew that this was in my future. I wished I knew what the purpose for this was, and where I was expected to go from here.

Journal
Chapter Four

A journal is more than a memory goad. It's therapeutic. The simple act of opening a notebook to put words down stills the crosscurrents of worry, drawing to focus the essential thought patterns that best define us, intersecting those thoughts with the condition of life at that exact moment. A journal is one of the few anchors the human condition allows us.
—Randy Wayne White (From Outside magazine)

Journaling has always appealed to me. I kept a diary as a young girl and carefully stowed away the key for the little brass lock that secured my innermost self. Over the years, journaling has served to help me metabolize what's happened in my life. It has been a way to transform what happens *to* me into my experience. Journaling has helped me integrate. This trauma experience was going to be a test of the healing benefits of 'putting it on the page.'

All through life, encounters and experiences happen. If they are not traumatic, then they are automatically assimilated. But when my life was affected by trauma I needed a way to integrate that experience into my life, into the history that is me. I believe that writing brought an understanding of my feelings and helped me deal with what was going on. It gave me a platform to make choices about how what had happened would affect my future.

Writing is a friend whose shoulder I can cry on. A journal is a confidant who listens and lets me sort things out. Journaling became the bridge that got me to the other side safely. It is a way to move from passive to active. I realized through journaling that I may have been the victim of circumstance but by understanding the circumstance better, I could place the event within the ongoing context of my life. Writing my thoughts down tells me that I am not powerless. Writing my thoughts shows me that I have choices and sometimes the recording of those thoughts tells me what those choices are. Writing my thoughts shows me when I am ready for change.

Looking back I saw the up and down of the process. I watched myself recover as I read the entries. I saw my struggle to cope as well as my strength. My healing was, and at times still is, a work in progress. Alone, putting ink onto the page, I often find that there seem to be other, higher forces that give me inspiration or insight. Whatever you feel comfortable calling the higher force, God, Spirit or the Universe seems to make it onto the page at those times when there is no one who can really do anything to help.

No matter what's happening, I always feel I have to try to act normal and not let others see what is really going on below the surface so they won't worry. There has to be some place where I can fall apart and be myself. For me, during the years after the accident, that place was my journal. It brought clarity and tenderness. Writing in my journal gave me a place to say, "I miss the old me." It gave me a place to say, "I'm afraid, I'm mad, I'm confused, I'm screwed," or "I'm grateful, I'm lucky, I'm blessed."

As I went back to my journals to do research for this book, I was struck by the feelings of loss and confusion that found their way onto the pages. Looking back at what I wrote was sometimes painful. At times I seemed to contradict my previous entry as I navigated my way into understanding. That was, and is, the importance of journaling. At the end of certain journal entries, I've noted lessons I had learned. They were moments when I 'got it.' Each was a valuable stepping-stone on my path back to *me*.

Journal Entry January 6, 1998

Wow! My first journal entry since I've been home and I have to admit a tantrum. Strong feelings always end up here, always have- -good or bad, it makes no difference. Yup! I had a temper tantrum the first week. I guess it was sparked by the frustration of being so immobile and the fear of being out of the rehab facility and on my own. Barry had gone out to run an errand. While he was gone, I had made a sandwich. I had rigged up a serving tray that I balanced on my walker in order to transport my meal to the living room sofa. On my way, I dropped the tray. My sandwich flew apart on the floor as our Golden Retriever, Flag stared at it, sensing that rushing to grab it was probably not in his best interest. I cried as I picked up the scattered pieces of bread and meat with the ever present claw. I put a cloth on the end of the claw and mopped the mustard up off the carpet the best I could. Flag ended up with the sandwich he had so smartly ignored and I went back into the kitchen to start over. All in all, the sandwich episode took about 45 frustrating minutes. I didn't realize how easy my life had been as an inpatient at the rehab hospital and for a moment, I wished I had my wheelchair back. I finally made my way to the sofa and ate my replacement sandwich, which had lost all its appeal. Barry came in not long after that with a crumpled fast food bag in his hand. He had been gone longer than I had expected and I had started to worry about him. (It seems that I worry about bad things happening all the time now.) I asked him where he had been and he said nowhere. I don't know if it was because of the way that he said it or because I had just had the sandwich episode, but I exploded. I was pissed that he had gone and gotten something to eat without even asking me if I'd like anything. He hadn't even thought about the gimp at home scrounging around in the fridge. Grabbing at everything with that damn claw, dropping things, re-doing tasks over and over, half the time exhausted just by doing the smallest chore. I yelled out, "Thanks for asking me if I wanted anything. I just finished dropping one lunch, making another and worrying about you because you had been gone longer than I expected, while you were out having a hamburger just to get away from me!"

I picked up my walker with my tray balanced on it and flung it at him. I was livid! He came toward me and I began to hit him, crying and telling him he didn't have to stay with me out of pity. He could divorce me if he wanted, I didn't care! He was trying to calm me down, telling me to stop before I hurt myself. He held me there, on the couch until I couldn't struggle any more. He had to be to work in an hour. I knew he didn't need to have this happen right before he left for work, but I was so miserable. I sat on the couch ignoring him until he left for work. Once alone, I thought about why that had happened and I realized that I was so damn frustrated and so humiliated by having to be taken care of. Barry has had to help me undress, wrap my cast so I can shower, and help me dress afterwards. Damn! I can't even roll over in bed without his help! I lay there like a beached sea turtle until he helps me turn over. I feel so useless, not to mention un-sexy, childlike, ugly, and generally a pain in the ass. I don't think I can do this much longer. I know he's ready for life to get back to normal, but it's still so abnormal to me.

Lesson:

Love yourself enough to push on when you want to give up and love others in your life enough to realize that they do not completely understand how you feel. Barry was probably relieved to have me home. I can picture him sighing with relief and thinking, *Oh good. She's home safe and sound. She'll be OK. I can finally relax and get a bite to eat!* To him, 'things getting back to normal' was a comfort. Things getting back to normal will come a lot sooner for those who love you than it will for yourself. Be gentle with those in your life who truly don't understand the complexity of what you are going through.

> *I learn by where I have to go.*
> —Theodore Roethke

> *One does not discover new lands without consenting to lose sight of the shore for a very long time.*
> —André Gide

Journal Entry: January 13, 1998

Frustrated-Frustrated-Frustrated!! I have no energy. I'm feeling more than the usual anger. The thankful, philosophical outlook I had in the first days after the accident is now only a distant memory. I'm tired of medication. I'm tired of trying to keep ahead of the pain. Sitting hurts, standing hurts, lying hurts, walking hurts, reaching hurts, bending hurts, showering hurts, rolling over hurts, being still hurts, moving hurts, existing hurts.

Maybe once I understand why I lived and what good has come,

I'll be able to actually feel the smiles I make sure everyone sees. Doctor appointment today. Hopefully good news.

I returned from the hospital about noon. The doc says that I can start therapy on an outpatient basis at the rehab hospital. I'm glad. I've felt lost and at a standstill physically. There is still so much recovery to be had. There have been improvements, but there is still so much I can't do. I don't think about it too much, because it scares me. Barry's at work, he'll call soon like always. I hope he stays with me, I love him so much. I'm so scarred up. I wasn't pretty to begin with.

Journal Entry: January 21, 1998

Pain's better. Glad for therapy. I'm free of the walker finally. I have a footed cane. I trip over the damn footed part mostly, but my shoulders don't ache as much as they did when I was using the walker full-time. I had a bath in my own tub!! It was a little tough getting in and out. I kind of have to roll over on my knees and lift myself out, butt up. It's definitely not pretty, but it's well worth the struggle. Baths may become my new favorite pastime.

Journal Entry: January 23, 1998

Well it looks like its all roses from here on out! Barring any unforeseen tragedy, all will be fine. I'll continue with therapy until mid-February. Aaron and I are starting to think about his graduation party. We've decided on an island theme, tropical, colorful, carefree. I have to appear as a witness in court on Tuesday. I'm a little apprehensive but I'll get through it.

Journal Entry: January 27, 1998

Useless trip to court as a witness. Charges were dismissed provided she never drives again. I didn't even get called to testify. I watched her family come in with her. They all clambered over me and the walker, maneuvering their way to the vacant seats in the same row. No one glanced my way. And worst of all, she never even gave me a sidelong glance. When I was in the hospital, I would sometimes wish I'd get an anonymous card in the mail so that I could assume it was from her and feel the forgiveness for her I knew I should. But the card never came, neither has the forgiveness.

I recognized one of the police officers that had been at the scene, sitting at a side table with other officers. The judge, the elderly lady and her attorney were conversing at his bench about how sad it was to get old and lose your freedom. The judge was telling a story about his mother and how she too, would soon lose that freedom. He was apologetic for her loss. I walked out of the court too stunned for any emotion. A young lady who worked at the mall came up to me and said she witnessed the accident, and if there was anything she could do, testify or something, to call her. She gave me a slip of paper with her name and phone number written on it. She said this wasn't fair. The police officer I recognized also stopped me outside the courtroom and asked if I was all right. I told him I was recovering. He said, "You get all you can out of this, you deserve it." I thanked him, because I didn't know what else to say. The tears came on the way to the car.

Lessons:

Life is not fair.
Forgiveness is always the right thing to do.
I learned about forgiveness that day in the courtroom.

I went home and wrote a letter to her, though it was never sent. I was so angry. In the letter to her I made sure to let her know how I felt about the way she didn't seem to care about what she had done. How hurt I was that neither she nor anyone in her family looked my way in the courtroom. The letter spoke of how her behavior toward me had taught me that no matter what, I would never allow myself to walk away from someone I'd hurt. I told her that I was hoping that the reason she didn't acknowledge me was because she had been advised not to do so, but that I wished she had gone against that advice. Then I told her I forgave her so that I could move forward in my life. I took a deep breath and at that moment made myself begin to forgive her.

I had to come to terms with forgiveness. I had to forgive those closest to me for going forward with the day-to-day normalcy of their lives while I hung back, seemingly stuck in recovery mode. I was trying to get back what I'd lost and they were speeding ahead. I had to forgive them because I felt lonely and left out. I had to forgive myself for my short temper, my frustration, and my lack of confidence in me.

Isn't it interesting how we usually use the words 'have to' with the word forgive? It's as though there is no choice. And there really *is* no choice if we want to move forward and be the best 'us' we can be. There is probably nothing more destructive than unforgiveness. It breeds resentment, bitterness, anger and hatred. Unforgiveness has no good use. And perhaps because it is so destructive, it is difficult to master.

> *What lies behind us and what lies before us are tiny matters, compared to what lies within us.*
> —Ralph Waldo Emerson

Journal Entry: March 4, 1998

At times I feel like I'm going crazy. I wonder if I need to see a psychologist. None of the doctors have suggested it. Is a person expected not only to cope, but also to figure things out on their own? I decided today that I needed to find something to read to help me deal with all of this. It was frustrating trying to find some emotional help for myself. Everyone listens when I need to talk, but I still feel so isolated, as if I'm in an unfamiliar country where no one speaks my language. There is an abundance of those daily devotionals/meditation type books but none appealed to me. I'm too frustrated to read beatitudes, platitudes and syrupy verse. Actually there was absolutely nothing for people who are recovering from the trauma of an accident, perhaps except for one entitled When Bad Things Happen to Good People, *by Harold Kushner, Rabbi. Bought it. I hope it will help.*

Journal Entry: March 6, 1998

I already devoured the book I bought just two days ago. It wasn't syrupy and actually helped. The author said what had to be true. Life was not fair. God was not the bearer of the chaos, and it does no good to ask "Why me?"--which is what I've already found out. According to the author, the question should rather be, "What now?" Of course it makes sense. I just need to know the answer. What now? And where do I go to find the answer? Perhaps it is just something I have to believe I'll understand one day.

Lessons:

I learned that 'what now?' is a question that can move you forward.

You won't have a different reality until you're ready to create it.

Sometimes I just had to keep putting one foot in front of the other and believe that it would be all right. The magic sometimes is just that we go on. Going forward, taking one moment at a time was all I could do back then. A great deal of 'what now?' has to do with thought patterns. Letting thoughts meander through my mind was not good for me. My mind was at times my worst enemy. While I was trying to be positive, often my mind would be filled with every negative possibility imaginable. Monkey mind, busy with everything but the present moment. When I found myself doing that, I'd stop and try to think purposefully. I know that thoughts affect the body. I know that my physical body does not differentiate between reality and imagination; just having a sad thought that causes your body to react is proof of that. I believe that choosing the thoughts I think, staying conscious and present in the reality of the moment changes the outcome of my future.

> *A great deal depends upon the thought patterns we choose and on the persistence with which we affirm them.*
> —Piero Ferrucci

Journal Entry: March 11, 1998

I went to a new doctor today. I'll be going to a different physical therapy facility. The doctor I'm seeing is a physiatrist, someone who specializes in physical medicine and rehabilitation. I'm feeling pretty depressed about all that I still cannot do. I'm still not back to work and I'm still in a lot of pain most of the time. I must continue to do the best I can. I am glad to be getting back into physical therapy because I feel as though progress has all but stopped.

Lessons:

Recovery requires activity.
Even small steps are steps toward recovery.

Determining to work hard at recovering what I had lost was my lifeline. I was still experiencing constant pain and stiffness. I never missed a physical therapy appointment and did every exercise as many times as I was told. I tried to swim laps (never have been able to do that very well), and I would tread water with flippers that felt like cinderblocks hanging precariously from my feet. I was bound and determined to make this thing work. The forward momentum of my physical capabilities started almost immediately. I began to believe that perhaps I could get back to somewhere near normal. Recovery hinges on our ability to go from thinking about what we'd like to see happen, into action to make it so. Recovery is sometimes two steps forward and one step back. I learned early that I could not hand the responsibility of my recovery over to my doctors, therapists, spouse, adult children or friends. Recovery had to stay in my custody, and sometimes it was lonely and frustrating. My recovery required that I put my blinders on and run my race. I couldn't compare my progress with anyone else's and I learned that I couldn't compare myself with what I was before the accident. I read recently that when an inexperienced horse is having difficulty running his own race, the trainer puts blinders on the horse so he cannot see the horses on either side of him and become intimidated or distracted. The horse with blinders is forced to see only what's directly in front of his own path. Put on your blinders and run your race!

In doing anything, the first step is the most difficult.
—Chinese Proverb

Journal Entry: March 20, 1998

Happy Birthday to me. Four months since the accident. I do have many things to be grateful for. As slow as it seems, I'm healing. The relief of it almost makes me cry. I cherish my family more now than ever and take pleasure in the smaller more ordinary things in life. I've come to know myself better since "we've" had so much time together! Ha ha. I really have wanted all this to accomplish something. In the beginning my anger had an activist energy and I wanted to lobby for legislation to keep unfit, older drivers off the road. But that faded with the forgiveness of the woman who accidently ran over me. I've learned so much about myself during this journey of recovery. I am amazed at the resiliency of the human spirit and in awe of the body's ability to heal.

Lessons:

Choose to be in a state of gratefulness and contentment. This opens the soul.

Have confidence in your ability to get through this.

Trust the spirit within you and the energy in the Universe. Quiet yourself so you can think. Pray so you can create with God. Be grateful that you are alive, that you have the opportunity to recover, and in the process you will learn much about yourself and the world around you.

Give up feeling sorry for yourself. Get busy doing the work of taking care of yourself, healing your body and mending your heart.

Many times during the years since the accident I've found myself angry again. I don't know if it's because the trauma I encountered was at the hands of someone else. I don't know if I'd feel differently if I had been rock climbing and sustained these injuries. But I would venture to say that it does make a difference inside when you're injured because of someone else's mistake. I think that the root of bitterness can get a better foothold under these circumstances and I have to be more vigilant about keeping it out of my life.

> *Yes, marks upon the flesh will fade, forgotten with the pain. But when the heart is wounded thus, the scar will long remain.*
> —Claire Richcreek Thomas

Journal Entry: September 15, 1998

So much has happened since my last entry – as always. In August we went to Myrtle Beach, just in time for hurricane Bonnie! Gees, don't know if God is trying to do me in or what? Just kidding. Well anyway, we were evacuated over night and had to sleep in a rest area because all the hotels were full. Needless to say, that wasn't the best thing for my recovering body! Some vacation!

August also brought a job change for me. I left the retail shop on the 22nd after trying for two months to work retail part-time. I couldn't stay on my feet for even four hours at a time and I knew this was putting an unfair burden on Maria. I began my new job on the 30th. I'm doing medical receptionist work for a physician. It's so miraculous because of what I wrote in an exercise I was doing while going through In the

Meantime *by Iyanla Vanzant. Taking something for sleep now to try to readjust my time clock. I've not slept well since the incident. It seems to have helped.*

Lessons:

Thoughts and words have the ability to create.
Never be too fearful to dream.
I feel as though I've become the self-help book queen of Albuquerque since the accident. I realize that some people don't want to dig into their psyches to try to figure out what they're feeling and why they are like they are. I am not one of those people. In this particular instance what came from my self-help sessions was nothing short of miraculous. You'll see as you read the rest of this paragraph why I say that. In one of the exercises from the book mentioned in my journal entry above, the author, instructed her readers to remind themselves of the experience they want to have in life. Do not set limits on yourself, just let your mind conjure up the best situation you can imagine, she instructed. (My paraphrase.)

I had been reading this book during the summer of 1998. During that time, I had been released by the physiatrist overseeing my rehabilitation to return to work part time. While working my first four-hour shift I found that I was struggling. I could no longer wear heels and stand for hours at a time. After that first four-hour shift, I hobbled to my car, which by the way, was **not** parked in the employee section of the vast mall parking lot, wondering how I was going to do this again tomorrow. Then I became concerned about how I was going to earn a living if I had to quit this job. All I had ever done since entering the work force was retail, and we couldn't make it on just one income. My heart was beating fast by the time I reached my car. I sat in my car and just cried. But I went back the next day and the next and the next.

During this time, I read the section in Vanzant's book about not setting limits on yourself, but instead just visualize what you want (sound familiar?). I did. Here is what I wrote that day for my answer to the exercise: *I want to have an enjoyable occupation. I love organizing and helping people. I want to work days only and have my weekends free. Oh yes, and holidays off* (who in retail doesn't?). *I picture an office setting, where I would be able to sit and stand at will so I wouldn't come home each day feeling like I'd been beat up.* Just days after writing my answer to the exercise I had an appointment at the doctor's office. While I was waiting to be called, the receptionist told me that she had put in her notice and asked if I knew of anyone who would like to work in the office. I surely did! And I knew why I would get the position.

> *Shoot for the moon. Even if you miss it you will land among the stars.*
> —Les Brown

Journal Entry: November 4, 1998

I began seeing a psychologist a few weeks ago. I was on my way to work on October 12th when I just had a meltdown. The air was crisp and the blue autumn sky was filled with colorful hot air balloons. Suddenly I just started to cry. I couldn't make myself stop. I wasn't far from my workplace, so that's how I came in that day, a wreck! The doc said that I'm suffering from Post Traumatic Stress Disorder (PTSD). He prescribed an antidepressant and visits to a psychologist. He said it was late in coming, but expected. It wasn't a good day. I feel as though I'm finally cracking! When my friend came to visit from Georgia, I was commended for my fortitude through it all and told how "great" I looked in this mushy, weakened body. I was secretly upset with her compliment though I smiled and said, "Thanks." I guess I just have no reserves left to cope with the upcoming anniversary of that day being so near. So much for superficial fortitude and the chin-up mentality I've been working so hard on!

Anyway, the psychologist has instructed me to walk Flag, once a week to lessen the paranoia and the feeling of panic that wells up inside me when I sense traffic behind me. Maybe the luxury of feeling safe around moving vehicles is gone forever. Maybe that's yet another thing to mourn.

This is not a very uplifting entry, but one good thing did happen. When I was at the psychologist's office the other day, she asked me if I secretly blamed my body for its struggle to heal and asked if I was I angry with it. A feeling of defensiveness rose up inside of me. My body? Angry at my body? Blame? I remember thinking. I explained to her that I was humbled by what my body had been able to accomplish. If anything, I felt that I had been overwhelmed by all the emotional ups and downs and felt like I had somehow let it down. I told her that, "No, *being angry or blaming my body was not something that I was having a problem with."*

Lessons:

Love your body enough to be patient with it.
Honor the process. There will most certainly be ups and downs.
Through the first weeks and even months of my recovery I viewed my body almost as a separate entity. I would speak to it as though it had a mind separate from mine. Perhaps that is what kept me from becoming angry at its slow progress, which in retrospect wasn't slow at all. What I now believe to be true is that it flourished because I had faith in its ability to heal itself. I was mostly in a quiet state of constant awe at my body's ability to heal. Such a humble mish-mash of tissue and bone, ripped, torn and broken; yet how brave and tenacious it was about healing itself! If my body wasn't going to give up, then neither would I. I promised it at the beginning when we put together our game plan, that I would do my part. Through the years since the trauma, I've continued to visualize my body as strong and capable even when I've been frustrated by the chronic pain and arthritic changes. I have much respect for the human body.

> *All sanity depends on this: that it should be a delight to feel heat strike the skin, a delight to stand upright, knowing the bones are moving easily under the flesh.*
> —Doris Lessing

Journal Entry: November 23, 1998

I don't know if anything will ever change the fear of traffic that I have or the vulnerability that wells up inside when I try to picture myself riding my bike or rollerblading. It's a terrible thought that anything similar could ever happen again. I just feel so lost and alone in all this. I know I have people who care about me and have helped along the way, yet here I am, feeling alone. Maybe because the first anniversary date is tomorrow. Maybe because I'm damaged forever. Maybe, maybe, maybe...

Lesson:

There will be times when you doubt your ability to continue. Know from my experience that you can.

After doubt, comes determination.

I remember waking up one morning in the hospital, not too many days after the incident and hoping, in those few seconds just before my eyes opened, that it had all been a bad dream and had not really happened at all. I remember the split second of hopefulness when my heartbeat sped up and my breathing increased with the anticipation of "it's only been a bad dream." In that split second I truly believed that it hadn't happened at all. Then I'd open my eyes as the fogginess of sleep lifted and I'd feel the sting in my nostrils and the tightness in my chest as my eyes welled with tears because I knew it was real and it had happened.

That moment of noticing how everything that defined who I was had now morphed into something/someone I was totally unfamiliar with, was sad. The feeling of loss was acute. After the moment of realization, though, the strength and determination would settle in and I would go on with the day.

> *There lives more faith in honest doubt...than in half the creeds.*
> —Lord Alfred Tennyson

Before I can share this next journal entry perhaps it would be helpful if I explained the meaning of the word descanso. Descansos exist in many cultures and regions throughout the world though I'm sure they are called by other names. They are symbols that mark a death, a place that speaks of remembrance.

Descanso is a Spanish word meaning *to rest* or *resting place*. They vary somewhat with region but usually they are symbolized by crosses that are often decorated with artificial flowers, ribbons that blow in the wind and things that sparkle and catch the glint of the sun. Some are flamboyant, others are subdued, just the little bare unassuming cross, hardly noticeable, sitting by the side of the road. I have lived in many places and I've seen them in the southern states, the southwestern states and even in Hawaii, draped with flower leis. A descanso says, "Right here, right on that spot someone's journey through this life ended unexpectedly."

Here in New Mexico I've seen descansos at intersections affixed to the traffic light poles, along isolated desert roads and on busy highways. I once saw a descanso along a pathway in the Rio Grande Bosque. It was a small cross nestled in the brush made from two small tree branches. There was a dog collar draped around the "t" of the cross. I remember wondering, "Had someone's pet died there at that spot, or was the descanso there to signify a favorite trail they walked together?"

Some descansos' ornamentation reveals much about the life it honors, others reveal nothing. But they rarely go unnoticed by me. In my breath there is always a prayer for the lives that were changed forever. Whether along desolate country roads, treacherous mountain roads, or sunny roads kissed by the salt of the Pacific, descansos have always made sacred a place of loss. Perhaps that is why that cold autumn morning, on the anniversary of the accident, I chose to place a descanso at that the exact spot where I was run over. It would be my way of signifying the change in my life, my private moment of memory.

Journal Entry: Tuesday, November 24, 1998

Last year on this date my whole life took a turn forever into a new uncharted place. It's early morning, about 3:30 a.m. and I'm going to the spot where the injury happened to try to gain some closure and perhaps to mourn quietly alone. I'm not sure what I'll do exactly, just that I feel compelled to do it.

The brisk November air swirled around me as I got out of my car in the vacant mall parking lot and walked to that very spot. I shuddered. I don't know if it was because of the cold morning air or if it was because I was standing in that place. I had written a note to myself. I set it on the pavement, lit a small candle and placed it on the note. The note read, "You did it. You survived. Continue to move forward. And even though you feel as though a part of you died here, there is also a part of you that is new. There is now a part of you that knows the depth of your strength. Be determined and you will continue to heal."

Huddled in my jacket, I sat on the curb and watched the small flame of the candle flicker in the breeze. It stayed lit despite the breeze and became a steady light where it sat in the darkness. I felt at peace there, watching that persistent little flame. There was a beauty about its confidence to exist alone in the vastness of the surrounding darkness.

I made positive affirmations in that place. I released the undeserved guilt I was carrying. Guilt, for perhaps thinking that something I had done or had failed to do had caused this to happen in my life. I thanked my body and spirit for getting me through this ordeal thus far. I thanked my God for being there for me to cry out to and though I'm not willing to believe that God is the one who takes or spares one's life, I thanked God for anything done for me in secret.

I drove away from that place with the little descanso flickering my determination into the early morning sky – my little beacon of courage and hope.

What I know about disappointment is this: A part of me was abducted that day on the cool autumn asphalt. I survived, but when I looked up, she was gone. The part of me that was athletic, strong and confident. Before the accident I had taught step aerobics and loved the challenge of weight training. I was pleased with how I looked at forty-one. I miss the person I used to be. Sometimes I'd sit next to where I think she is and it makes me sad. I'm sad because of the sense of loss I feel without her. I miss what we were together. I had a glimpse of her the other day when I was riding my bike at lightning speed down a flat stretch of the bike trail, weeds bending with the breeze of my tires as I passed. I could feel her excitement and her strength and I knew that it was not only me that day on my bike, but us.

> *You need only claim the events of your life to make yourself yours. When you truly possess all you have been and done, which may take some time, you are fierce with reality.*
> —Florida Pier Scott-Maxwell

Unmourned disappointment stops progress, and since life is never really at a standstill, regression happens instead of progression. That is the reason I chose to spend that moment with myself at the place of the incident. I didn't want to become a victim of the loss. My desire was to thrive and become a better version of me.

Journal Entry: Thanksgiving morning. November 26, 1998

I'm grateful that I'm here. Grateful for the opportunity to continue my life. Now let's see what I can do with it.

Ponderings

Unsolved matters are like a pebble in the shoe.

Gratefulness makes warm, the cold places in the heart.

Peace is not a matter of choice as much as it's a matter of necessity.

Courage is fear's shell.

Time spent alone is to the soul, what a warm candlelit bath is to the body.

Journal Entry: February 15, 1999

Since the accident, at times my personality has ricocheted from one end of the spectrum to the other. It's been frustrating not only for me, but for Barry as well. Healing is a present moment activity. My energy needs to be focused on the 'now.' I can't allow myself to be triggered by uninvited thoughts that contort and distort who I am. During the first week of my stay in the hospital I listened to my intuition because I couldn't do anything else but think and listen to what was inside. During the last few months I've become defensive and depressed because I've forgotten to continue to visualize my healing process. I must stay in the present and not allow past woundings to have a place in my present. I must not dwell on the future's uncertainty and allow myself to be swallowed by imaginary mishaps. I have every reason to be proud of the things I've accomplished thus far. I've made it, and will continue on. My body is different now and I accept that. But I also believe that my body is still healing and can still become better.

Lessons:

Getting over the trauma is not the goal. Integrating it into the fiber of your self is the goal.

Examine what is true about you.

What are your expectations for yourself?

What are you willing to do to successfully achieve them?

When you seem to plateau in your recovery, rest in that place. Stillness is not inactivity.

Integration is the process of making what happened to you a part of the history of your life. This process removes the trauma as a stumbling block and instead allows it to be used as a foundation block for the changes you have experienced. You can find peace by reminding yourself of the kind of experience you want to have. How do you want to feel right now? Next week? Next month? In one year? In five years? Doubts will arise as you examine what is true about you and what you'd like to see in your future. Doubts are normal. Don't let them stop you from continuing to visualize what you want to happen.

I used my soul/spirit as the source when I envisioned what I wanted to be the outcome of this event five years down the road. I had no reason for choosing five years, but I remember lying in my hospital bed and thinking to myself, "What do I want that time to look like? I believe the vision I had of myself came from my soul/spirit that night when I was thinking about my future. That vision then caused me to act in a certain way; this became my *mindset* during recovery. The thought from the soul *set the mind* so that the vision could become a reality.

How do you change your mind? Change where your thoughts go for direction. The thought is the action that changes the mind. The soul/spirit is the reservoir for hope, faith and intuition. Take your thoughts from your soul's hope chest and act on those thoughts. Write down simple, attainable goals so you'll have something to work toward. Then write down your successes so you can see that you've had some.

What have I learned about myself? I've learned that I can be strong. I've learned that I don't have to be strong. What have I learned that does not work? Guilt does not work. Regret does not work. Living the past over again in my mind does not work. Wondering why this happened to me does not work. Putting myself down does not work. Seeing only the bad in me does not work. Blaming others, God, or life does not work.

> *Trust that still, small voice that says, "This might work and I'll try it."*
> —Diane Marie Child

> *No trumpets sound when the important decisions of our life are made.*
> —Agnes De Mille

GRACE
CHAPTER FIVE

Faith is nothing but a living, wide-awake consciousness of God.
—Gandhi

Living in Grace-Living in the Present

Many years before the accident at the mall, I had an experience that was life altering. I was going through a rough time in my life and I was worrying about the future way too much. I was upset and crying as I drove down a country road in Georgia. In my frustration, I complained to God about a situation coming up that I was dreading and all that was unfair in my life.

"Stop!" a voice from somewhere commanded. I was so shocked that indeed I did stop. I also nearly ran off the road. I pulled over and looked in the back seat to see if someone was there. It continued, "Stay in the present, this moment. Grace is sufficient for today. When you allow your mind to time travel into the future or the past then you leave the covering of grace. Nothing exists but now, the present moment. Today, all is well. When the day you are dreading arrives, you will be allotted the portion of grace for that day."

And that was it. The voice was gone. I can't be sure if the voice was truly audible, but it was so powerful internally that I could 'hear' the words. I have never forgotten that experience.

During my stay in the rehabilitation hospital the words I had heard years before were once again brought to the forefront of my mind. I decided then that I would do my best to stay in the present during my recovery. I believe that there is a Source Energy/God in the universe. What that Source Energy is called is different for the different peoples of the world. I cannot discount this God Energy in my recovery. In the book, *When Bad Things Happen to Good People*, Rabbi Kushner posed a question that left an indelible mark on my life. He states, "We can redeem these tragedies from senselessness by imposing meaning on them. The question we should be asking is not, 'Why did this happen to me? What did I do to deserve this?' That is really an unanswerable, pointless question. A better question would be 'Now that this has happened to me. What am I going to do about it?'"

I have spent the years since the accident trying to focus on "What should I do now?" rather than "Why did this happen to me?" When I look back, I can see that I was allotted my portion of grace for each day. I can see that even journaling was a way of grace; in that it brought about understanding of my life for each day. The wonderful people who came into my life at different times, each bringing a different talent, were the keepers of the grace for each day and led me along the path to healing. Here's an example of that.

In April 2001, three years and five months after the

accident, I remember still feeling oddly disconnected from the world at times. It still felt as though my body and spirit were not functioning as one. I didn't know what to do to fix how I was feeling. A friend who had been instrumental in helping me gain spiritual and physical mobility through T'ai Chi Chih, a form of moving meditation, mentioned a weekend retreat she thought would be helpful to me. I decided to sign up and try it.

I left for my adventure on late Friday afternoon. I turned off the two-lane highway onto the dirt road to the address on the pamphlet. The home was situated on a few acres of land outside the city limits in the quiet, open space of New Mexico. The scent of piñon pines, mesquite and chamisa filled the evening air. As I pulled up to the house, I still wasn't sure that I'd made the right decision, but I had decided that I would be open to the journey of the weekend.

I was welcomed inside, met everyone and the trek through our psyches began. After we were all situated we were given an overview of the retreat schedule and led through some exercises which were intended to help each of us find the answers and healing we were seeking. I won't go into detail about everything, but it was a weekend of guided and unguided meditations, walks, writing/drawing exercises, talks, and a sweat ceremony with a Lakota woman on the last morning. It was a weekend that opened up a possibility to me that I had never considered.

On the first night we were guided into a meditation practice in which we made ourselves small and went into our heart. We were told to use our imaginations and picture that place. After the meditation we each drew a picture of that imagined place. My drawing was a depiction of myself as very small, standing in a forest with an upside down rainbow underneath me. When I looked at my finished drawing, I wasn't surprised by the feelings it evoked in me, small, lost and the world turned upside down.

The last day of the retreat a time was set aside for individual counseling. When it was my turn, she led me through a guided meditation in which my vivid memory of the accident came into question. She told me that she believed I had not been 'alive' the whole time during my memory of the accident. She said that the drawing with me standing on the upside down rainbow was evidence of a split in my spirit/body. Had I been conscious throughout the accident or was my vivid memory of each moment under the car the result of my watching the accident outside of myself? Had my spirit separated from my body for a time? Was that the reason I had been feeling separate from myself and disconnected from humankind? Questions swirled through my head at that moment as she guided me into a meditation that was meant to bring wholeness of body and spirit.

As the years have passed, I truly can't say for sure whether I had a moment outside of myself and that is why I have this vivid memory of the accident, but then again, there had been no proof that the 'voice' I'd heard many years earlier was real either. There is more to the world than what we experience with our five senses. I believe that I've had help along the path to healing. Sometimes my angels dwelt inside my spirit and sometimes they were the compassionate human angels that came in and out of my life at just the right moment along the way.

THRIVE
CHAPTER SIX

*The thing of course, is to make yourself alive.
Most people remain all of their lives in a stupor.*
—Sherwood Anderson

Surviving is Good-Thriving is Better!

I made a decision along the way to live better than before the accident. I didn't want to be someone who had just survived a trauma, but rather someone who had learned to thrive because of what had happened.

I still use parking lots, which, I guess is equivalent to getting back on the proverbial horse. The sound of a vehicle behind me as I walk still makes my heart beat fast and I turn toward it, just to make sure the driver sees me. They are quirks that I have now. They're not huge. I can now say that I'm grateful for the many changes the accident brought to my life. The decision to be grateful allows me to thrive.

The choice to thrive washes over those who love us. Barry never told me I wasn't going to get better. He always believed that I would get through. In retrospect I realize that he helped me to thrive. He's the stereotypical male who is not excessively verbal with his feelings, but he always told me that everything would be all right, and when I felt I really couldn't handle it anymore, he was always there. One of the personality traits I enjoyed most about him while we were dating was that he liked to joke and tease. He didn't stop teasing me for long, just because I was injured. As a matter of fact the words 'speed monkey' still make me smile. He used to call me that as I maneuvered with the walker.

"Come on, little speed monkey!" he'd tell me as I made my way between house and car or down the hall, or out in the back yard. It became a joke between us.

It was those silly little interactions that made up for all the things he didn't understand or didn't say when I thought he should have. I wanted to thrive because of him, because of humor and life and happiness. And there was a part of me that felt it very important that he be proud of me. I think he is, though he's never come right out and said it. (It's a guy thing, as my eldest son likes to remind me).

Learning to thrive takes time. It sat below the surface of my being while I processed all that was involved in the trauma, the physical, emotional and spiritual. I've tried to pin down when it actually emerged. There was no 'ta-da' moment. It was more of a continual choice, like deciding each day to be content or grateful or to smile.

Live

Chapter Seven

If we take care of the moments, the years will take care of themselves.
—Maria Edgeworth

In ending, I would like to add that I realize that there are people who have survived much worse traumas than I – horrendous things that I know must be tremendously hard to live through. I am humbled by the sheer strength and determination of these individuals. I realize that they have learned things through their experiences that I did not because I was able to recover almost all function. Yet through the years since the accident I've had the opportunity to work in the medical field with physicians who specialized in both pain management and rehabilitation, and I've learned that how a person goes forward after a trauma is truly up to each individual. I have witnessed people who have gone through far less than I did, and whose lives have been thrown into a tailspin because of a traumatic accident. I've determined it's what happens inside to propel a person through the pain, fear, self-pity, doubt and anger that brings about the resolve to recover as best you can.

This brings to mind a conversation I had with Maria (my co-worker from the mall) one day while she was visiting me at the rehabilitation hospital. She was telling me with tearful eyes that she didn't know how I could do all the things I was doing. She said that she could never be as strong as I had been. I know that she meant what she said as a compliment, but it kind of irritated me when she said it. I remember telling her that I'd had no choice. I could curl up in the corner and die or I could fight like hell to get my life back. What choice did I really have, but to recover?

Were there times when I felt hopelessness, self-pity, anger, bitterness and the unfairness of the situation? I did! I shared only a few journal entries in this book, but there were many entries throughout the years. Sometimes I was so mad when I wrote that I tore the pages out and threw them away. The first two years were hard for me. I had made the decision early on to stay away from narcotic medication, and therefore had to become creative in order to manage the pain. I worked at keeping myself busy doing what I could to distract myself from the pain. I went back to work as soon as I possibly could because I needed to feel productive, and work kept me from dwelling on myself and ruminating on the past that I had no power to change. When I realized that I couldn't do one type of exercise I'd try another. I became aware of how different my body was now from what it had been before the accident, and I've tried my best over the years to try to figure out what works best for me. As I age, I realize that it will always be a work in progress and that's fine. I had a lot of angst the first couple of years because I couldn't get back into the running, weight training and step aerobics I had been using to work out before the trauma. My body just fought my attempts to get back into those forms of exercise. I don't know why, but it did. So over the years

I've taken up different forms of exercise like, yoga, spin cycling and walking. I want anyone who reads this book to know that recovering well is definitely one hundred percent doable and you are the only one who can do it. Work at finding what's best for your body. Be kind and patient with yourself along the way.

I believe that if I had stayed at the wallowing hole drinking the muddy waters of resentment, anger and self-pity, my body would have been poisoned by the murky water I had lapped up and would not have been able to heal as completely as it did. I would have killed every good and abundant thing in my life if I had not determined to come through this experience as best I could.

At the beginning of this book I stated that by writing my story I hoped to gain insight into myself, to find my purpose and place in a world that chose to spare my life. 'What now?' became the prayer for my life and this is what I've determined is my answer. I was spared and chose to heal to the best of my ability so that I could:

Let my husband hold me as I sobbed; frustrated, frightened and tired from the fight.

Have this many more years to love him and him me.

See my youngest son graduate from high school and grow to be a man.

Take my turn, as my dad lay dying, to tell him one last time that I love him, that I was so glad that he was my dad and that he could go now, reassuring him that it was all right. We'd all be OK.

Send care packages to my eldest son as he served as a soldier in Iraq.

And be at Fort Riley when he returned home so that

I could hold him and look into those eyes that I wished had not seen any of the pain and fear they'd witnessed.

Sit on my porch during a quiet spring morning sipping coffee, writing in my journal and feeling the breeze, scented with the perfume of Spanish broom mingled with honeysuckle.

Spend time with my close friend, Corona in hand, on a warm Florida night as we laughed and talked of life, as only girlfriends can do.

And finally, write this book in the hope that others who struggle with the shocking 'what now?' of a traumatic experience will also be encouraged, gain insight into their healing process, and realize that the reason they were spared was so that they can truly live.....

Just to be alive is a grand thing.
—Agatha Christie

Good Reads

Here is a list of some of my favorite 'spirit food' books. I believe that as sentient beings we are connected, and that we affect one another with our words.

When Bad Things Happen to Good People by Harold S. Kushner

Write It Down, Make It Happen by Henriette Anne Klauser

In The Meantime by Iyanla Vanzant

The Seat of the Soul by Gary Zukav

Happier Than God by Neale Donald Walsch

Change Your Thoughts - Change Your Life by Dr. Wayne W. Dyer

The Power of Now by Eckhart Tolle

The Beethoven Factor by Paul Pearsall, Ph.D.

Women Who Run With The Wolves By Clarissa Pinkola Estés, Ph.D.

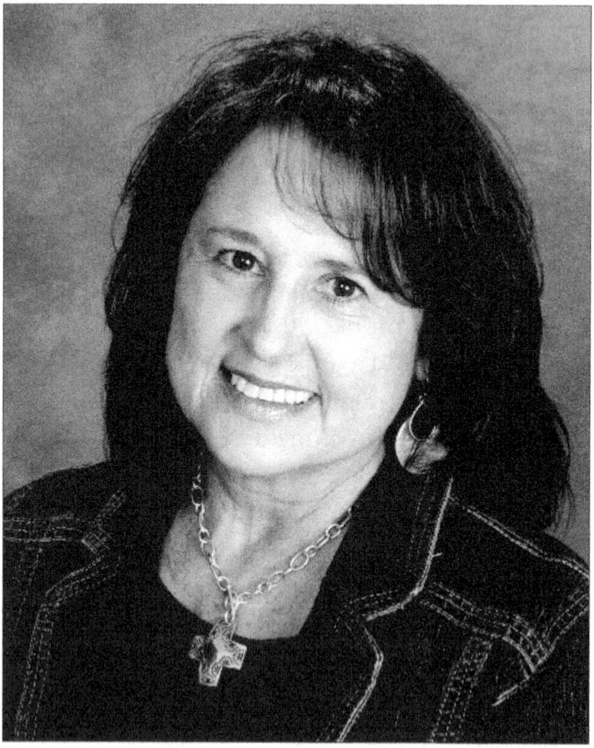

About the Author

Alice Hurst currently resides in New Mexico with her husband. Since the accident, she has worked with various healthcare facilities and was a licensed massage therapist for several years. Because of her life changing event, she has become especially interested in the mind, body, spirit connection we all share, and seeks to contribute in a positive way to our collective human experience.

Colophon

The typefaces used in this book are California FB (TrueType), Kozuka Gothic Pro (PostScript), and Trajan Pro (PostScript). Book designer Stewart Warren used several Adobe Creative Suite applications including Photoshop and InDesign.

Made in the USA
Columbia, SC
28 June 2021